I Wonder Why

Farm Animals

Karen Wallace and Nicki Palin

KINGFISHER

NEW YORK

Copyright © 2009 by Macmillan Children's Books
KINGFISHER
Published in the United States by Kingfisher,
an imprint of Henry Holt and Company LLC,
175 Fifth Avenue, New York, New York 10010.
First published in Great Britain by Kingfisher Publications plc,
an imprint of Macmillan Children's Books, London.

Distributed in Canada by H. B. Fenn and Company Ltd.

Library of Congress Cataloging-in-Publication Data has been applied for.

ISBN: 978-0-7534-6285-0

Kingfisher books are available for special promotions and premiums.
For details contact: Director of Special Markets, Holtzbrinck Publishers.

Printed in China
10 9 8 7 6 5 4 3 2 1
1TR/0908/MPA/UNTD/157MA/C

Consultant: David Burnie

Contents

Sheep

Many different animals live on a farm. Sheep live outside in the fields all year round, eating grass. Their woolly coats keep them warm. The farmer brings the sheep inside only when they have lambs.

shearing (cutting off) a sheep's coat

sheep in a field

4

1. What is a fleece?

2. Why do some sheep have colored spots?

3. What helps a farmer move his or her sheep?

fleece

sheep with no coat

1. A fleece is a sheep's woolly coat. It can be made into wool.

2. Some farmers paint spots on their sheep so that they can find them if the sheep get lost on another farm.

sheepdog

3. A sheepdog runs around to help the farmer move the sheep.

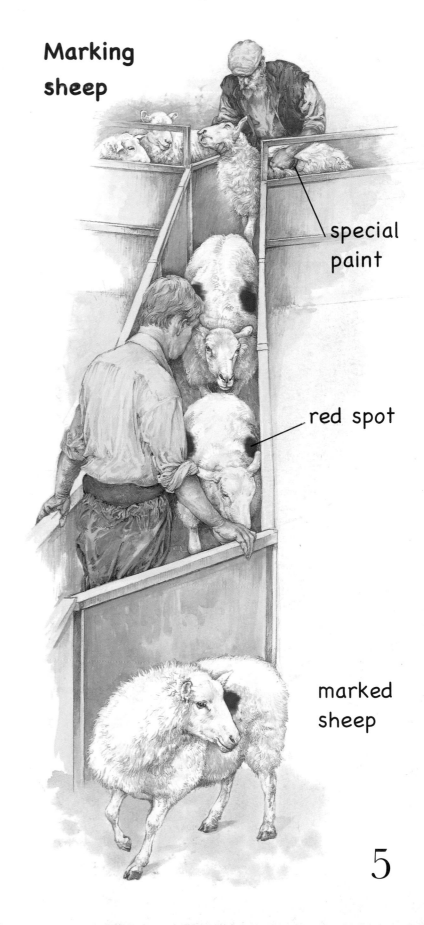

Marking sheep

special paint

red spot

marked sheep

5

Pigs

There are many types of pigs. Some pigs are huge and spotted. Others are brown or black and white. Most farmers keep large, pink pigs because they have a lot of piglets and produce good meat.

pig warming up in the sunshine

mother pig sleeping

6

1. How does a pig stay cool?

2. What do pigs eat?

3. How many piglets does a mother pig have?

cooling down in some mud

nine piglets drinking
their mother's milk

1. A pig rolls in mud to stay cool and protect its skin from the sun.

2. Pigs eat a mash made out of barley and wheat. They also like cabbages and other vegetables.

3. A mother pig has around eight to eleven piglets.

mash from a feeder

vegetables from a trough

cabbage from a bucket

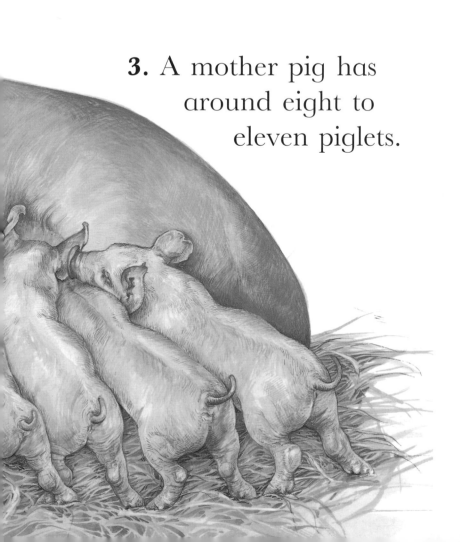

Goats

Goats do not like being alone, so they stay together in a group, called a herd. Most farmers keep goats for their milk, which they make into cheese.

herd of goats in the mountains

**kid
(a baby goat)**

horn

beard

two male billy goats

8

1. Do goats live
in the mountains
all year round?

2. What keeps
goats happy?

3. Why do goats
have horns?

goats on the farm
for the winter

billy goats
butting horns

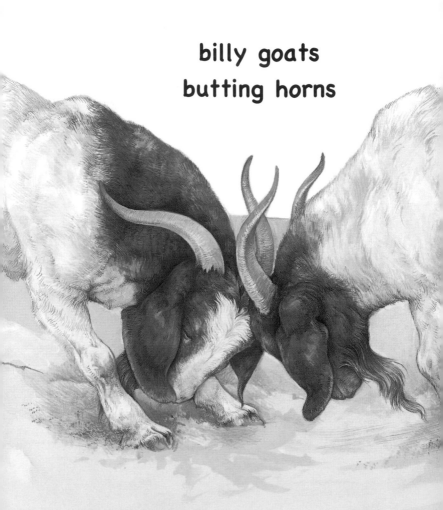

1. Some goats graze in the mountains in the summer. In the winter, they move down to the farm.

2. Goats like plants to eat and space to play. They also like to sleep.

Goats enjoy . . .

eating

playing

3. Goats use their horns to butt each other when they are fighting.

sleeping

Chickens

At night chickens sleep
in a special house to keep
them safe from wild animals.
In the morning the rooster
wakes them up with a
loud cock-a-doodle-doo!

chicken scratching
the ground

rooster
(a male chicken)

10

1. Why does a chicken scratch the ground?

2. What type of feathers do chickens have?

3. Why does a mother hen sit on a nest?

hen
(a female chicken)

feeding a worm
to the chicks

keeping the
eggs warm

1. A chicken scratches the ground with her feet to find insects and worms to eat.

2. Chickens can have short or long, fluffy or spotted feathers. Roosters have long tail feathers.

3. A mother hen sits on her nest to keep her eggs warm and help them hatch.

Some types of feathers

fluffy feathers

spotted feathers

rooster

long tail feathers

11

Cows

Many farms are home to a large herd of cows. In the summer, the cows live outside in the fields and eat grass. Baby cows, called calves, live with the herd.

herd of cows eating grass

calf drinking its mother's milk

12

1. What do cows
eat in the winter?

2. Why do farmers
keep cows?

3. How does a
farmer get milk
from a cow?

cows eating hay inside a shed

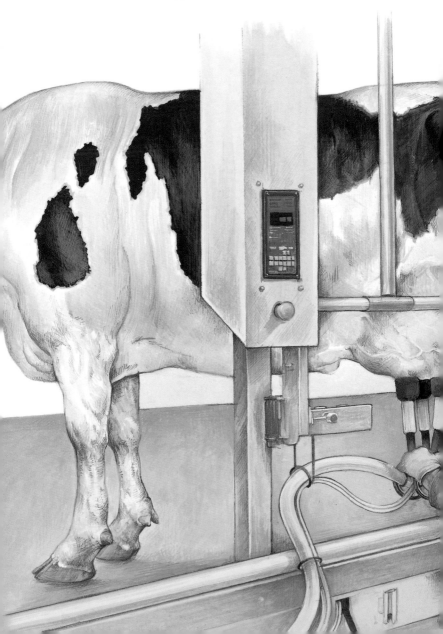

1. In the winter, cows eat hay and grain. They live inside a shed.

2. Farmers keep cows for their meat (beef) and milk. Milk can be made into cheese, yogurt, and butter.

3. A farmer uses a milking machine. It has special tubes to suck out the cow's milk.

using a milking machine

Some foods from cows

beef pie

roast beef

hamburger

milk

cheese

yogurt

butter

13

Horses

On some farms, horses pull carts or help plow fields, but on most farms, horses do not work. The farmer and his or her family enjoy taking care of the horses and riding them across the fields.

horse wearing
a bridle

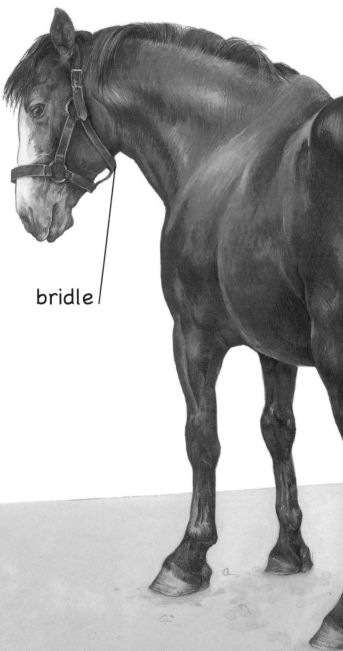

bridle

tools for
taking care of
the horse's hooves

14

1. What is a bridle?

2. Are there many
types of horses?

3. Why does a horse
wear shoes?

fitting
a horseshoe

hoof

1. A bridle is a set of leather straps for a horse's head. It helps control the horse.

2. Yes. There are big and small horses, spotted horses, and racehorses, which gallop very fast.

3. A horse wears metal horseshoes to stop its hooves from wearing down.

horseshoe

Some types of horses

Shire horse

Shetland pony

Appaloosa

racehorse

15

Ducks

Most farmyard ducks have white feathers and orange beaks. Mallard ducks, which are wild, are different colors. They visit farms to build a nest beside a river or pond.

cleaning feathers
with beak

female duck

male duck

webbed
foot

mallard ducks
swimming in
a pond

1. Why does a duck clean its feathers?

2. When do ducklings hatch?

3. Why do ducks have webbed feet?

shaking out old feathers

1. A duck cleans its feathers to stop them from soaking up water when it swims. Then it shakes out old feathers.

Ducklings hatching

Ducklings grow inside eggs . . .

2. Ducklings hatch after they have grown inside an egg for one month.

and then the eggs hatch.

3. Ducks have webbed feet to help them paddle around and dive underwater.

nibbling plants at the bottom of the pond

The ducklings soon learn to swim.

17

Index